Your Friendly Neighborhood Hope Shop

Love, Blessings
2021
and Hope!

Marolyn Mustra

Your Friendly Neighborhood Hope Shop

An Advent Devotional

Rev. Mandy M. Mastros, LSW

ACADEMY
PRESS

For permission requests, write to the below address:

Mandy M. Mastros
PO Box 1327
Lancaster, PA 17608

The opinions expressed by the Author are not necessarily those held by PYP Academy Press.

Ordering Information: Quantity sales and special discounts are available on quantity purchases by corporations, associations, and others. For details, contact the author at pastor@lancastermoravian.org.

Edited by: Cathy J Frey
Cover design by: Ann R. Malcolm
Typeset by: Medlar Publishing Solutions Pvt Ltd., India

Printed in the United States of America.

ISBN: 978-1-951591-80-9 (paperback)
ISBN: 978-1-951591-81-6 (ebook)

Library of Congress Control Number: 2021912210

First edition, October 2021

The mission of the Publish Your Purpose Academy Press is to discover and publish authors who are striving to make a difference in the world. We give underrepresented voices power and a stage to share their stories, speak their truth, and impact their communities. Do you have a book idea you would like us to consider publishing? Please visit PublishYourPurposePress.com for more information.

PYP Academy Press
141 Weston Street, #155
Hartford, CT, 06141

Table of Contents

Introduction

Danny* came into the church office looking for a bus pass, as so many do. Our conversation started with the familiar request, followed by my customary: "Tell me a little bit about you." That is where the routineness ends. Each person's response to that question is as unique as a sunrise or a snowflake. Sure, there are themes, often a combination of adversity, pain, loss, resilience, and courage. However, beyond the theme, each person's story is different and so is the way the teller chooses to share it with me.

Danny told me that he was homeless, his wife was in the hospital for an infection, and he wanted to go see her. Could I give him a bus pass? We talked for a bit about how they had ended up on the streets and what his hopes and plans were to get off the street. I offered him a snack and a bottle of water. I gave him an all-day bus pass to get him to the hospital and back to the shelter. Before he left, I asked him the same closing question that I ask everyone who comes into the office: "Are you a hug or a handshake kind of guy?" He, like 90% of the others, opted for a hug. As he walked out the door he smiled and said, "Thanks for letting me shop at the Hope Shop."

I am deeply humbled, and often in awe of the vulnerability of people who meet me for the first time and share openly of themselves and their hurts, of their mistakes and their losses, of their struggles and their hopes. Time and time again, that simple question opens the door to a deeper conversation, one that leads us into a relationship that goes beyond the need for a bus pass, a snack, or some toiletries. I have learned to never underestimate the value of giving a person a safe space, a listening ear, and an invitation to share his or her story.

The people sharing these stories have seen and experienced so much hardship, and yet, through our conversations and relationships, I have had encounter after encounter that has left me hopeful and blessed by some of the most beautiful people I have ever met. Often there are no easy answers or quick fixes for these individuals. Most of those who come into my office are homeless and will still be sleeping on the street after they leave. Church staff, volunteers, and I do what we can with material resources, and we make referrals to and give out information about community programs that may be more equipped to help with tangible needs. We always try to do this in a way that is welcoming, nonthreatening, and nonjudgmental.

It is always my sincere desire that each person leaves with a bit more hope than when that person came in the door, but the truth is, those who come to shop at the Hope Shop often leave a payment of hope that equals or exceeds what they took with them. I could tell you story after story of the ways that these individuals have touched my life in deeply powerful ways. Actually, that is exactly what I am going to do. As we enter this season of Advent, a time of hopeful expectation, I invite you to read on, ponder, reflect, and pray, as I share with you 25 stories of Hope Shop customers.

*All names have been changed.

"Let's put it on the pastor's tab!"

Scripture Verse: "The eye is the lamp of the body. So if your eyes are healthy, your whole body will be full of light." – Matthew 6:22 (NRSV)

Story: I have learned that it is never a good idea to work out a mental to-do list before I go into the office. That's exactly what I was doing on this February morning as I walked up the sidewalk. I stopped to greet a man standing outside, and he asked how I was doing. I responded and asked the same of him, and when I looked at him, he held my gaze a bit longer than normal. I knew he wanted to say something else, so I smiled at him and waited. He said, "Do you have a dollar or two, that I might be able to get breakfast at McDonalds?" I replied, "I don't carry cash on me, but I would be happy to buy you breakfast here at this sandwich shop." He quickly turned me down, saying that the sandwich shop was too expensive, and he could not ask that of me. I told him he wasn't asking, I was offering. And if it made him feel better, we could just put it on the pastor's tab from the church next door. I was sure she wouldn't mind.

He looked at me strangely but followed me inside and got in line. He ordered his sandwich and while we waited, I asked him some questions to get to know him better. He told me his name was Juan* and that he was homeless. He had been on the streets for a couple months. I asked if he wanted to bring his breakfast to my office, and maybe we could explore what housing or shelter options might be available for him. He seemed eager. We walked to the church, and he questioned, "We're going in here?" I said, "Yes, I work at the church." When we got to my desk, I handed him my card and explained that I was the pastor and was happy to see what we could find for him. He chuckled, and his smile grew wider as we got to work.

We called to do a homelessness intake, to check on the status of his insurance, and to check on his Social Security benefits. When he was on hold, which was often, he'd tell me a bit more about his story. Where he'd made mistakes. Where he'd struggled to get back on his feet, and all that he had lost in recent years. With each call he remained calm and patient, even when asked repeatedly for his address and phone number although he had told them he was homeless. Juan was transferred to more than a half dozen individuals and was on the phone for more than two hours. He was more patient with the people he spoke with than I would have been.

Reflection: Juan was such a kind and gentle person to work with. He didn't want to be a burden. The look in his eyes said he wanted to ask for help when I began talking to him, but he would not have asked if I had not given him the opportunity. By lingering for that extra moment, I gave him the time to gather his courage to ask for help.

Ponderings: Have you ever hesitated to ask for help because you were embarrassed or afraid? When/if you did ask for help, what made it possible for you to overcome that fear or embarrassment?

Prayer: Jesus, help us to look into the eyes of others in a way that sees what their lips are not saying. Help us to see you in those eyes and respond in the way we would respond to you. When others look into our eyes, may they see your love and kindness reflected in them. **Amen.**

"Come on up. We're eating now"

Scripture Verse: "For if you love those who love you, what reward do you have? Do not even the tax collectors do the same?" – Matthew 5:46 (NRSV)

Story: It was a typical Sunday morning worship service followed by cookies, coffee, and conversation. The message had been about the Good Samaritan. While a few of us were talking about the message as we waited in line to get our snacks, I looked up and saw one of our members who had just left return. Behind her was a man in a wheelchair. He had a prosthetic leg, and he was missing an eye. She guided him to a corner of the room where he could plug in his wheelchair to recharge and then she came to me. She said, "I was on my way out of the building and Ralph*asked me for a few dollars to get something to eat. I didn't have any cash with me, but I said, 'Come on up.

We're eating now.' I didn't think you'd mind." I assured her that I absolutely didn't mind, and I saw her actions as a modern-day example of the Good Samaritan. She served him a plate of food, and I watched as a few of our congregation members went over to engage him in conversation.

I learned a bit of his story in subsequent weeks. Because of the kindness he was shown on that first encounter, Ralph has returned multiple times. One week I went to get him a plate of food, only to find that someone else had already put one together for him. Another week I walked into our worship space and he was perusing the library while seated in our transport wheelchair. One of our members had pulled it out for him so that he could recharge his chair during worship but not be stuck sitting in the corner. How thoughtful! I have enjoyed watching the ways in which the rest of our church family interacts with this man. It all started with a simple request and a loving response.

Reflection: Our member who initially engaged with this man could have said, "I'm sorry, I don't have any money" and kept walking. She didn't. She could have walked past him and ignored him. She didn't. While she could not meet his request for cash, she took the time to meet a deeper need, and from that kindness, several relationships were formed. Not only did this woman form a connection with Ralph, but so did some of the other people from the church.

Ponderings: When in your life has a simple interaction turned into an opportunity for an ongoing relationship?

Prayer: Dearest Jesus, when you told the parable of the Good Samaritan to those early followers, it was to help them understand who their neighbors were. Help us to remember each and every day that any human being who crosses our path is indeed our neighbor. We may not be able to meet everyone's needs, but help us to honor their humanity and do whatever we can. **Amen.**

"You remembered my name....
Thanks for being nice..."

Scripture Verse: "But now thus says the Lord, he who created you, O Jacob, he who formed you, O Israel: Do not fear, for I have redeemed you; I have called you by name, you are mine." – Isaiah 43:1 (NRSV)

Story: It was time for our monthly prayer walk. Someone suggested we go to the Towers, the high-rise apartment complex just a couple blocks away. On a bench outside sat a man with a large duffle bag sitting open next to him. We went to say hello. I noticed the vodka bottle only half covered in his bag. He told me his name was Dennis.* He was waiting for his SSI benefits, and then he would be able to get off the street. We offered him a blessing bag, and he was very grateful. We talked a few more minutes and offered him communion, which he politely declined. We wished him well and went on our way.

The following month as our walk took us past the Towers, we again spotted Dennis sitting on the bench. I said, "Hi Dennis, how are you?" He said, "You remembered my name! Wow!" He quickly tried to cover up the open vodka bottle in his bag. I told him it was OK. He didn't have to hide it on my account. A few minutes later, he told one of our walkers how impressed he was that I had remembered his name. We offered him a blessing bag, and he told us he didn't need the whole bag but could use some snacks and socks. We all rummaged through our bags and gave him two bottles of water, three pairs of socks, and a few snacks. He marveled at our generosity. A week or so later, I was driving by and stopped at a red light next to his bench. I rolled down my window and yelled, "Good morning, Dennis." He smiled and waved. The next day, he got up off the bench and came to my window. He said, "Thanks for being nice. Most people aren't very nice to me." I told him that I was truly sorry to hear that, and I promised him that I would continue to wave, beep, or offer a word of greeting whenever I drove by. The light turned green, and he thanked me again as I drove off.

Reflection: I have had to train myself to remember names because it doesn't come easily to me. Often our brains are two steps ahead of the conversation, causing us to miss an initial introduction. Names are important because they let people know that we see them as unique individuals. The people who live on the street often feel invisible. Calling them by name not only makes it clear that they are seen, but also that they are remembered.

Ponderings: Think about a time when a person you hadn't seen in ages, or a person you had met only once or twice, remembered your name. How did it make you feel? What does it mean to you to know that God calls you personally by name?

Prayer: God of many names, thank you for remembering my name. Help me to remember that you know even the most intimate details about me and my life because you desire to be in a deep and personal relationship with me. Remind me that you love all of your children with that same kind of love, and help me to love each one too. **Amen.**

"Food has power; power to start wars and to stop them"

Scripture Verse: "At twilight you shall eat meat, and in the morning, you shall have your fill of bread; then you shall know that I am the Lord your God." – Exodus 16:12 (NRSV)

Story: Often times at the community breakfast provided by Anchor Lancaster, a non-profit organization in Lancaster, Pennsylvania, I take a few minutes to talk with the director of the program. During this time, I check in with her to see how she is doing and how the program has been going. I ask if there is anyone who really needs someone to talk to, and we compare notes about some of the individuals we work most closely with. I love to see the way the guests of the breakfast program interact with her. For the most part there is a gratitude and a respect for this ministry that provides a hot meal to so many. Individuals are invited to eat as much as they want. For some, this may be the only meal they get that day.

One day, when talking about the program, Tyler* told me how important it is to get a good breakfast. He said, "Most folks don't realize it, but food has power. It has power because it is something we all need. People fight over resources like food. Food has the power to start wars and to stop them." I stood there marveling at this man's insights. He was so unassuming in his speech. He went on to say, "I think if we could find a way to make sure everyone had enough food to eat, we'd also have peace in the world." My first instinct was, "What an idealistic but lovely thought," but the more I pondered, the more I realized that this man was on to something. What could we do in a world of satisfied stomachs? If we could find a way to work together to meet this basic human need for all people, how could peace not follow?

Reflection: Tyler experiences hunger regularly, and he spends much of his time with folks who also experience hunger regularly. Because of this he has insights into the power of food that most will never be able to articulate. His specific life circumstances make him an expert on the power of food. While societally we tend to live in a scarcity mindset, there is more than enough money and resources in the United States to end the problems of poverty and hunger. If we could find a way to come together and make that happen, the world would improve in miraculous ways!

Ponderings: I invite you to think about meal times when you were a child. How did your family's food practices influence your current relationship with food? What power or influence does food have now?

Prayer: God of the abundant harvest, you have given us everything we need to live, love, and grow together as your children. Help us to identify places where we are not being good stewards of the resources you have entrusted to us. Help us to fight for food security for those who experience hunger. Help us to work for justice in all areas where people do not have what they need to live and thrive. Teach us creative and meaningful ways to harness the power we have for your glory. **Amen.**

"Look D., this says I'm a beloved child of God"

Scripture Verse: "Look with wonder at the depth of God's marvelous love that has been lavished on us! God has called us and made us God's very own beloved children." – 1 John 3:1a (TPT)

Story: One of the ways that our congregation engages with and offers support to individuals in need in our community is through blessing bags. Each small cloth knapsack contains a bottle of water, a few snacks, some toiletries, and socks. In the winter months we add hats, scarves, and gloves. We keep a supply of these bags in the office for people who drop in, but we also take some with us on our monthly prayer walks, a time when we walk through the streets of our city praying for those who live, work, and play here. We often tuck little notes into our blessing bags. They are just a simple message of encouragement: "Smile, God Loves you" or "You are God's beloved child" or "I'm praying for you today." It's an important way to help supply physical items of support as well as a little spiritual pick-me-up.

During one of our prayer walks, we strolled through Binn's Park, known by many to be a hub for drug activity and a place where individuals suffering with addiction and addiction-related issues often hang out. (There have been many discussions among community leaders about how best to help the people who hang out there.) We approached a few individuals and exchanged greetings. We asked how they were doing and listened as they shared parts of their stories with us before offering them blessing bags. Diana* and D.* accepted bags and thanked us.

Immediately, Diana started looking through the contents, "oohing" and "aaahing" over the socks and the granola bar with a big smile on her face. Then she pulled out a little pink card and read it out loud with confidence. "I am a beloved child of God. Oh, wow!" She nudged the guy sitting next to her and said, "Look D., this says I'm a beloved child of God. I know that's right. Mmmhmmm, yes, I'm God's daughter." Diana turned to me and said, "You know, I'm gonna be baptized at this church next month, on the 16th. That's right! I know my God loves me, and this card reminds me of that. I'm gonna keep this." She sat the bag down next to her and hugged that little pink card to her chest. Then she got up and hugged me and everyone who was part of our group that day.

Reflection: In a bag full of tangible practical items, the one that caught Diana's attention was a simple pink index card with seven words written on it. Human beings are multi-faceted creatures with multi-faceted needs. Addressing the physical need is important, but equally and sometimes more important are the needs that can't be seen with the naked eye.

Ponderings: When is the last time someone did something for you or said something to you that spoke to a need for connection or belonging to God or to others? How did that impact you?

Prayer: Multi-faceted God, you have created us in your image, a beautifully woven design of body, spirit, and soul. Nurture all of our many dimensions and help us to nurture others in that same way. Help us to remember that we are your beloved children, each and every one of us, and help our words and actions remind others that they too belong to You. **Amen.**

"How can I pray for you?"

Scripture Verse: "We always give thanks to God for all of you and mention you in our prayers constantly." – 1 Thessalonians 1:2 (NRSV)

Story: My car died. I could have arranged for a rental while I looked for a replacement, but our church is right above the bus station. It seemed frivolous to do anything other than take the bus, even if the bus stop is a mile from my house. I took the Route 10 Lititz bus to and from the office maybe half a dozen times over the next two weeks. On several of those days, I sat across from a man named Frank.* Frank was a talkative man, and he saw my pleasant greeting as an invitation. Perhaps it was.

Each time we had a variation of the same conversation. He asked me questions: "What is your name? Where are you going? Why are you taking the bus? What do you do for work? How much school did that take? Were you good in school? Did you watch the football game?" Each time after the litany of questions, he'd say, "Could you pray for my kidneys? I got bad kidneys." I would agree to pray for his kidneys, and then he'd ask me to pray for his wife and her health concerns and his daughter who "wasn't doing too good." After he exhausted his list of prayer concerns, I'd offer to pray with him there on the bus, and he'd say, "No, can you just do it at the church?" I'd agree.

After a brief pause, Frank would say, "And pastor, how can I pray for you?" The question caught me off guard every single time. At first, I thought about brushing it off and telling him I was fine or telling him to pray for the church and the people there. But here was a man who wanted me to pray for his kidneys, for his daughter who was never "doing too good," and on one occasion, for his little dog. He was looking for a connection. So, I'd tell him something that was going on in my life that he could pray for. Once it was that I would find the right car. Once it was for Edna, my dog, who had a vet appointment because she had been bitten by a skunk. After each of these encounters as we would get off the bus, he'd shake my hand and say, "You remember to pray for my kidneys, and I'll pray for your car (or for your dog, or whatever I had requested)." I promised that I would, and I thanked him for his concern and his prayers.

Reflection: When a person finds out I am a pastor, it is not unusual for them to share a prayer request, or two or ten, with me. It is rare, however, for them to offer to pray for me. Whenever this happens, I try to take that offer as seriously as their request for prayer.

Ponderings: When has someone offered to pray for you? How did that make you feel?

Prayer: God who hears, we thank you that you listen to the prayers of your people equally, regardless of their vocational calling. Thank you for the Franks of the world who remind us that it is good and right to ask others to pray for us and for us to ask others how we can pray for them. We thank you for the power that comes when two or three are gathered together and ask for anything in your name. **Amen.**

"I actually got off my butt and did something..."

Scripture Verse: "Whatever your task, put yourselves into it, as done for the Lord and not for your masters, since you know that from the Lord you will receive the inheritance as your reward; you serve the Lord Christ." – Colossians 3:23–24 (NRSV)

Story: Luann,* Vera,* and Dana* came to the office because Luann and Vera needed to get photo identification cards. Luann had her ID, but it had expired. Vera's ID had either been lost or stolen. Dana came along because she had nowhere else to be. I asked Luann to come to my desk so we could see what we could do. Hers would be easy, requiring just the entering of a few numbers and changing an address. She asked me if we could have it sent to the Water Street Mission, because she had nowhere else to receive mail. I assured her that we could do that. While I worked, she told me that she had left everything and gone to the Mission because her boyfriend was abusive, and it wasn't safe to live with him anymore. She said she had gotten to the point where her life was more important than any of her earthly belongings. I encouraged her, and offered words of affirmation regarding her decision. She told me she believed God was with her in the process.

Vera's story was a bit different. She looked worn, but pleasant. She tried to keep our conversation light, even as she told me that she had struggled with drugs and for a long time would do anything to score. She was clean when she came to see me, and she talked about how hard that was. She wanted to stay clean, but she couldn't find the motivation to do much to get her life put back together. She was staying at the Mission, but felt as if every attempt she made to improve her life had failed. She said she wouldn't have come for her ID that day if Luann hadn't been coming, but since they were hanging out together, here she was. She enthusiastically took a prayer rock off the table in the office and asked if she could keep it. Maybe it would help motivate her to pray. Both girls prepared to leave with prayer rocks and their temporary ID cards in hand, as well as the assurance that the permanent ones should arrive at the Mission within a few weeks. As they were waiting for the elevator, Vera said to Luann, "I finally got off my butt and did something for myself, and look, it worked," holding out her temporary ID. I could hear the excitement in her voice.

Reflection: Sadly, Luann's story is not unique. The struggles of starting over after an abusive relationship are multi-faceted and can include finding a new place to live, a job or source of income, enough clothing, new ID cards, and other important documents. Luann was afraid that the man who abused her would come back and hurt her again. Sadly, that is a common and very real fear for many survivors of intimate partner violence. This is even more complicated in families with young children. Getting away from the abuse is one of the first and most important steps, but also one of the most difficult. Taking those first steps, the ones that may seem simple to an outsider, can be hard. Life on the street is often met with rejection and failure, which can be incredibly demoralizing and demotivating. My hope for Luann and Vera is that they can find the courage to take the steps to do what God is calling them to, and that they feel God's presence with them as they do it.

Ponderings: When have you struggled to find the motivation to do something you needed to do? What was the catalyst you needed? How did it feel when you accomplished your task?

Prayer: God of the depressed, the weary, and the unmotivated; God of the abused, the scared, and the brave, we ask that you pour out your comfort and grace on all those who have experienced or are experiencing the pain of intimate partner violence. Provide wisdom on how to exit these situations safely. Stir an attitude of compassion and grace in our hearts for those who have given up and need support and help to take even the first baby steps on the road to putting their lives back together. **Amen.**

"I was wondering if you had any clothes"

Scripture Verse: "Forty years you sustained them in the wilderness so that they lacked nothing; their clothes did not wear out and their feed did not swell." – Nehemiah 9:21 (NRSV)

Story: A dear friend of mine was struggling. Her children and her husband's children lived in Florida. Due to issues of declining health, they decided that it was time to move from Pennsylvania to Florida to be closer to their children. An avid shopper, she had amassed a lifetime of things, clothes, shoes, and accessories. She needed to downsize significantly. She asked if we collected clothing at the church. I told her that we didn't because of space restrictions, but if she wanted me to, I would take the clothes to the Food Hub. She was exceedingly grateful the day I showed up and filled my car with bags of clothes, linens, etc. I looked through each bag and pulled out socks, gloves, cardigans, and other items I thought we might be able to use in the office or the adult day center. I noticed there were several bags of men's medium- and large-sized clothes, including at least a half-dozen nice sweaters and a few heavy winter coats.

The next day I bumped into Joshua,* a gentleman I had worked with previously, sitting outside the church. I asked Joshua how he was doing, and after we talked a while, he asked if I knew where he might get some clothes. He was in need of some warmer items now that the weather was changing. I told him we didn't usually provide clothing, and was on the verge of recommending some locations that do when I hesitated. "What size do you wear, Joshua?" "Medium or large," he answered. "Of course you do," I chuckled, explaining to him the events of the previous day. We marveled for just a moment at the timing of it all, and then made an appointment for him to come by the next day. He left with a big bag of almost brand-new sweaters, pants, and a new jacket. I wanted to help one friend, but God provided an opportunity for me to bless a another as well.

Reflection: When we look for God and are tuned in to God's movement in our lives, we are more likely to see God's presence. In our fast-paced society, we are often distracted and miss these regular appearances of the Divine. She can appear in big and life-changing ways, but also in the simple or even the mundane.

Ponderings: How do we decide when something is coincidence or when it is "Godincidence"? What can you do to be more tuned in to the subtle or not-so-subtle ways that God works in our everyday lives?

Prayer: God of all time and space, help us to recognize the ways you pop into our lives unexpectedly. Keep us focused on you so that we are more aware of your movement in and around us. Thank you for blessing us with ample opportunities to be a blessing to others. In Jesus' name, **Amen.**

"I can't tell you where I was... I have to go there tonight!"

Scripture Verse: "For the greatest love of all is a love that sacrifices all. And this great love is demonstrated when a person sacrifices his life for his friends." – John 15:13 (TPT)

Story: Self-preservation and loyalty to others are important values to have when you find yourself on the street. Ironically, the programs and systems that are set up to help individuals can cause problems for those who are seeking assistance. The individuals who navigate the system quickly learn to spot these flaws. They adhere to the unwritten rule: Care for oneself and for each other.

I was helping Clarence* walk through the phone intake process to get him admitted into some type of shelter. The woman who was interviewing him asked him where he had slept the night prior. His answer was vague, and she asked him to be more specific. He again skirted the question, and she explained that she needed to enter an answer into the computer. Finally, Clarence replied, "I'm sorry, but I can't tell you where I was. I found a safe place to sleep with a few other people, and if I tell you, and you tell the police, they will come and make all of us leave. Then none of us will sleep tonight." She accepted that answer and moved on to the rest of her questions.

After Clarence got off the phone with her, he tried to explain himself to me. "I didn't mean to be rude or to lie, but if they can't get me off the streets today, I don't want to give up my spot for tonight and I don't want to mess it up for my friends either." I assured him that I understood, and that I had no intention of reporting him, or even asking specifically where he was going to be. Before I started having regular conversations with unsheltered individuals, I assumed that it was every man or woman for themselves out there. I have since learned that exactly the opposite is true. When we give someone a bus pass or a blessing bag, or when we help someone to get their photo identification card, often that individual will return with a friend so that the friend can get help too. Whenever someone tells me that Clarence told them to come see me, I smile and feel relieved, knowing that this person has a reliable and loyal friend.

"I can't tell you where I was... I have to go there tonight!"

Reflection: Whether you have extremely limited resources or all the resources in the world, having a loyal friend is an irreplaceable blessing!

Ponderings: Who would stick by you when things are difficult? Take a moment to thank God for that person or persons. Take a moment to reach out and thank them for the gifts they are in your life.

Prayer: God of relationships, thank you for putting people in our lives that we can depend on. Help us to acknowledge and appreciate those relationships more fully. Make us loyal and trustworthy companions to those we interact with each day. God of the lonely, provide a friend and support to those who do not feel as if they have anyone they can depend on. Dependable, reliable God, help us to remember that you will never betray or deny us and that we can always turn to you. **Amen.**

"I NEED HELP!"

Scripture Verse: "Everyone sees my life ebbing out. They consider me a hopeless case and see me as a dead man. They've all left me here to die, helpless, like one who is doomed for death." – Psalm 88:3–4 (TPT)

Story: It was my first day back after vacation. I was feeling refreshed, but also a little worried about all that awaited me on my desk and in my email. I approached an intersection just a few blocks from the church and saw a man standing on the corner. He was holding a sign that said, "I NEED HELP." I saw him standing there, but was a bit relieved when I realized that the light had turned green and the traffic behind me would make it unsafe for me to stop. Half way down the next block I heard a voice in my head telling me to go around again. I argued with the voice. "Really? I'm just getting back. Can't I just go to the office?" However, I did obey the voice and I went back.

I pulled up next to the man and rolled down my window. I said, "Hi, I'm Mandy." He told me his name was Bo.* When I asked him what kind of help he was looking for he said, "All kinds really. I live in a little apartment just up the street by myself, and I'm just having a hard time trying to figure out how to make it all work." I explained to him that I did not keep resources in my car, but I would be happy to work with him if he was willing to come to my office. I handed him my business card and told him that I would be available in the morning every day that week. He did come by the office at 3 o' clock that afternoon, smelling strongly of alcohol. I wasn't free to work with him that afternoon, so again I instructed him to come back in the morning, writing my office hours on the card I had given him.

The next morning, Bo came by and shared a bit more of his story. He is an alcoholic with significant anxiety. His insurance copay is too expensive to afford the appointments with his psychiatrist, so he self-medicates with alcohol. He talked about his times in and out of rehabs and psychiatric hospitals, and said he couldn't figure out why it never stuck for him. With desperation, he said, "I am so anxious I can't leave the house sometimes, except if it is to go and get a drink, because I know the alcohol will help me feel calm enough to be able to be out in the 'real world.' I need someone to help me figure it out." We talked more extensively about his needs for community, for social connection. He was quite articulate about his needs and desires. By our second appointment, although his situation hadn't changed, he was ready to take some action steps toward healing: talking to his landlord, making payment arrangements for a couple of bills, and making a game plan for the next couple of days. Bo is a delight to talk to because he truly isn't looking for someone to live his life for him. He just wants someone to walk beside him through this tough patch.

Reflection: My spiritual director has told me in the past that sometimes we need to encounter Jesus with skin on. This sounds like what Bo so desperately needs. He believes in Jesus' saving power. He believes that Jesus is with him on his journey, and he would like a person to walk with him too.

Ponderings: Walking alongside someone is a very powerful way that we can be witnesses to God's love in this world. Have you ever been that person for another? Has anyone ever been that person for you?

Prayer: God, who relinquished supreme power by taking on human form and walking among us in your great living example, you have shown us how to come alongside those who are sick, those who are hurting, and those who are lost, and reach out our knowing, compassionate, helpful hands. Help us to live into this example, so that we may accompany people on their journeys in the ways you taught us. **Amen.**

"But he didn't do anything wrong"

Scripture Verse: "Whatever happens to one member happens to all. If one suffers, everyone suffers, if one is honored, everyone rejoices."– 1 Corinthians 12:26 (TPT)

Story: It didn't take long for the ladies at the sandwich shop down the street to realize what I was doing when I came in to buy a meal for a hungry person. They started plugging in their employee discounts when I brought a new person with me for food. Over time, I learned more about them, and they learned that I was the pastor from the Moravian Church. I was out of the office one day when Donna, a staff person from our church, called to ask if I might be able to help her with something. She said that Melissa,* one of the cashiers from the sandwich shop, had come to the church looking for assistance for one of her customers.

Mario,* a man wearing a protective helmet, had come into the restaurant with a man who bought him something to eat and then left. Mario had removed his shoes, eaten his meal, and fallen asleep. Melissa could tell there was something wrong, but she did not know what to do. She told Donna that she didn't want to call the police because the man hadn't done anything wrong, and she didn't think they would be kind to him. Donna went back to the restaurant with Melissa to talk to Mario. He explained that he wore the helmet because he had a traumatic brain injury and was a fall risk. He had come in on the bus from New York the night before and had spent the night in the emergency room due to some health issues. He was in town to see his daughter, but she did not know he was coming. He planned to go to the shelter for the night and was heading there when a stranger offered to buy him a meal. His feet had swollen a great deal and they were hurting him, so after he had eaten, he slid out of his shoes and dozed off. When he woke up, his feet were too swollen to put his shoes back on. He was feeling vulnerable in the city and was not sure what to do now that his shoes were too tight. He didn't think he could walk to the shelter. After hearing this, Donna called me to ask if we might be able to locate a pair of bigger shoes.

It just so happened that earlier that day, I had gone to an event hosted by the city's Food Hub, formerly known as the Lancaster County Council of Churches. At that event I had met the woman who handles their clothing distribution program. She had given me her card and told me to call her if she could help me with anything. I called her, and she told me she would see what she could do for Mario. Happily, they had a pair of shoes in a bigger size, and Donna was able to pick them up while Mario waited.

And just like Cinderella's glass slipper, the sneakers were a perfect fit. Mario looked up at Donna and said, "You are angels. I don't know how I ended up in the right place at the right time, but I did." He reached into his bag and gave Donna one of the gifts originally intended for his daughter. We don't know how his reunion with his daughter went, or if it even happened, but what we do know is that he saw a messenger of God in the kindness of strangers and a pair of sneakers.

Reflection: There is power in teamwork. When we work together, we can do more. I think about all the people who worked together to help Mario that day, and I see the power of community. One stranger bought him a meal; Melissa from the restaurant came to the church to seek help for him; Donna called me; I called my contact at the Food Hub; and she provided Mario with shoes that had been donated by yet another person who played a vital role in this story.

Ponderings: When have you worked with others to help meet the need(s) of someone in your community?

Prayer: God of connections, help us to remember that all of creation are bound together by your love and grace. Open our hearts to collaborate and cooperate with others so that we may find ways to serve our brothers and sisters in our neighborhood and in the world. Guide us to the people we are called to work alongside and give us courage to step out and connect with others, knowing all the while that they too are your beloved children.

"I know I belong to God, that's how I know it's going to be OK"

Scripture Verse: "Jesus said to him, 'I am the way and the truth and the life. No one comes to the Father except through me." – John 14:6 (NRSV)

Story: Misty* came into the office after encountering Sally,* a woman on the bus who has been coming to our church for quite some time. Sally had recommended that Misty come talk to me about what was going on in her life. Misty was feeling depressed and anxious. She had a history of alcoholism and had been clean for just a couple of months. She was living at the shelter, but was not getting along with some of the other women there. Misty told me that she reads her Bible each night. She had just read the passage about Jesus' being the way, the truth, and the life, and she believes that to be true. In her heart, she believes that everything is going to be OK. She just needs to keep pressing on and keep trying to do right by God. I prayed with her, and I continue to pray for her regularly. I want it to be true, to believe that someday, on this side of glory or on the other, everything will be OK for her. I know that alcoholism and drug addiction, while not nearly as powerful as God, are painfully challenging to overcome.

A few short weeks later, Misty relapsed and began drinking again. Unfortunately, or perhaps fortunately, her probation officer found out pretty quickly. Misty was mandated to a rehab facility and then to a halfway house. She visited me during her stay at the halfway house and shared what had happened. She's been sober for several months and still holds onto her faith. At the same time, she still fights with depression and a desire to numb the pain in some way. The last time we spoke, she told me that her belief in God is what keeps her going. She said she has considered suicide, but believes that God put her here, so who is she to think she can decide otherwise? Her daily struggle is real. Staying clean and staying true to her faith are difficult for her, but she hasn't given up yet.

Reflection: One of the things I love about Misty is her honesty. She knows that God loves her on her good days and on her bad days. She believes that God wants her to share what is going on in her life with God, even when her thoughts are not pretty. She didn't clean it up for me. What she shares when we talk and pray is real and sometimes ugly, but it is genuine, and I can't imagine that God would want it any other way. If we believe God is the way, the truth, and the life, we can know with certainty that the way to a better life is by sharing our truth with God.

Prayer: God of Truth, help us to be honest with ourselves and with one another about our shortcomings. Give us courage to speak about our shortfalls and struggles without beating ourselves up about them. Remind us that you know the most difficult and ugly details of our lives, and even those are covered by your amazing grace. There is nothing we need to hide from you. Help us to trust others with our stories so that our relationships with them may grow and deepen. **Amen.**

"This don't feel like no church"

Scripture Verse: "Discover creative ways to encourage others and to motivate them toward acts of compassion, doing beautiful works as expressions of love. This is not the time to pull away and neglect meeting together, as some have formed the habit of doing. In fact, we should come together even more frequently, eager to encourage and urge each other onward as we anticipate that day dawning." – Hebrews 10:24–25 (TPT)

Story: I was standing outside the church talking to Tabby,* a woman I had previously worked with. She had two friends with her, and I invited all three to come inside. We took the elevator up to my office, and I gave them each a bottle of water. Kim* noticed the bowl of prayer rocks sitting on the table and asked if she could have one. While they were each picking out a rock to take along,

I asked Junior* to tell me a little bit about himself. He said that being out on the street was way better than what his life at home had been, which was not a testament to how good it was to be homeless, but rather to how bad his homelife had been. He shared more deeply with me, and I found myself moved by his vulnerability with me, a complete stranger.

His friends interrupted us, and Kim asked me what time church started on Sunday. Junior looked at me skeptically, "This is a church? I don't go to churches. I mean, no offense, but you don't want me in your church, the building might burn down or something. I didn't know. This sure don't feel like no church." I assured him that it was indeed a church and that I was the pastor. I also told him that I don't believe that God punishes people by striking them with lighting or causing them to perish in a fire. I shared that I believe in a God who loves all people no matter where they are from, what they do, or how they feel about God. I also assured him that I wasn't offended by his comment; if his past history with churches caused him to be concerned about hellfire and damnation, then I was grateful that we did not feel like a church to him.

This opened up the conversation even further, and Junior shared that because his childhood had been so difficult, he struggled to believe that God could possibly love him. And if God did, how could God allow him to suffer so much? I told him that I understood how he could feel that way and reassured him that his reaction was normal and that God understood too. After a few more minutes Junior said to me, "I know this is a church, but as far as churches go, this one isn't so bad. Maybe I could come back sometime."

Reflection: There are so many people out there who struggle with going to church. The reasons vary, many because of something that a person in or associated with the church has said or done to them. Others are angry with God. Perhaps they feel as if God has abandoned them or caused or allowed a specific hardship to happen to them or to a loved one. Whatever the cause, these feelings are real and valid. The best thing we can do when talking to persons who are struggling with their relationship is to validate their feelings and let them know that our caring about them is not contingent upon their involvement in any type of church. Perhaps you have been hurt by the church or someone in it; above all else know that you are loved by a God whose heart breaks when people suffer, especially when done in God's name.

Ponderings: Have you ever doubted God's love for you? Have you ever avoided church or church activities because you were angry or afraid of God?

Prayer: God of those inside and outside the church, we pray for your peace and blessing upon all those who have been hurt by the church. We ask for opportunities for reconciliation when helpful. We ask for open hearts and minds to hear these stories without judgement. Help us to remember that you are just as present with those who talk about you in coffee shops and in their homes as you are with those who gather in more traditional worship spaces. **Amen.**

"If you want to help the homeless, talk to my pastor"

Scripture Verse: "Do not withhold good from those to whom it is due, when it is in your power to do it." – Proverbs 3:27 (NRSV)

Story: One night, a group of people gathered for a Narcotics Anonymous meeting in the basement of a nearby church. It was an open meeting, which means that anyone may attend regardless of their history with addiction. This is where Jenny* and Brad* met. Brad has been clean for a year. Jenny has never used, but feels God is calling her to do some sort of ministry with those in need. Her passion is for the homeless, but she realized that having some experience with individuals coping with addiction would probably be helpful. Brad had come to our church for rental assistance, food, financial counseling, and referrals to other community programs. He also attended our church service a few times, but not with regularity. Brad came to this particular NA meeting every week, never missing. He liked the people there. Jenny had been attending regularly for several weeks when Brad approached her.

He said, "You know, if you really want to help the homeless in this community, you should talk to my pastor. She really helped me when me and my woman were gonna be out on the street. She works with people all the time. That church did a lot for us too, gave us lots of stuff we needed when we got into our apartment." Jenny took down my contact information and sent me an email. We met one day for coffee, and she shared her story with me. She is happily married with two grown children. She has a good paying job and enjoys her life. She likes her church and was not looking for a new church family. She was simply looking for a place to plug in, to connect with the homeless in the city, and Brad led her to us. Jenny now donates items to our blessing bag ministry, works with us on our brochures, and comes along on our monthly prayer walks. She stops and prays with people on the street and adds her voice to our petitions for those who work, live, and pray in our city.

Jenny's heart is for ministry to those whose needs are related to poverty and homelessness. Obviously, so are Brad's. He didn't have to offer to connect Jenny and me, but he did. The last I've heard he's still clean, but his struggles with poverty and homelessness have continued. Sadly, embarrassment has kept him away from the church, but the brief time that he was in touch with us had a positive impact on him and on us.

Reflection: Brad's invitation to Jenny on our behalf has been a blessing all around. The affirmation that we are a good place to go if you want to help persons experiencing homeless in our community reassures us that our work is not in vain. So often we see people once or twice, offer assistance, pray with and for them, but never know if we have made an impact. It's hard work, but we have to trust that if we are truly following God's leading in our service, our work is making a difference. Brad's invitation blessed us, it blessed Jenny with an opportunity to 'plug in' to the community in a new way, and it continues to bless those who now receive Jenny's aid.

Ponderings: Have you ever felt like you were in the right place at the right time because of God's leading or nudging? How have those moments impacted your life?

Prayer: God of interconnectedness, we marvel at how you bring people together in the right places at the right times. We thank you for Brad and for Jenny, and for all those who encourage others to work together for your good. We ask that you give us the courage to do what is right, even if we may never know the impact of our words and actions. Help us to trust that all things done in your name and for your glory are working together for your good in this world. **Amen.**

"Drugs before family, food, and God"

Scripture Verse: "You shall have no other gods before me." – Exodus 20:3 (NRSV)

Story: Oscar* and I were working to get him into a shelter. He didn't have a phone, his insurance had been cut off, he had HIV and hepatitis, and he was estranged from his family. We completed the United Way 211 assessment and applied for his insurance reinstatement. We were waiting for the callbacks. Oscar was incredibly patient with all of the individuals he talked to, even when the insurance agent repeatedly asked for his address and phone number. I marveled at his composure, feeling myself get angry on his behalf. He didn't falter. While we were waiting to get our callbacks, Oscar said he was going to go get some air, and he'd be back within the hour. He didn't return.

The next day, Oscar came into my office with blood-shot eyes, looking very disheveled, and said, "I'm sorry I didn't come back yesterday. Will you still help me?" I said that I would, and he said, "I don't need housing, what I really need is rehab. I left here yesterday feeling overwhelmed, and I spent the night using. I'm so sorry. Will you still help me?" Together we started making phone calls. When asked specific questions about his drug use, Oscar said, "I use whatever I can get my hands on, whenever I can get my hands on it, and as much as I can get my hands on." The last time he had used was just two hours ago. We succeeded in getting his insurance reinstated, then we started looking for a bed for him at a rehab facility. We learned that there might be something available, but we would have to wait for another callback.

Oscar said he would go and come back. I was concerned, so I asked him, "Oscar, do you feel like you can safely go and come back without using?" He looked at me with the most serious expression and said, "Pastora, I have put drugs before mi familia, food, my health, and my God. I am ready to get help and I will be back here by four o'clock." He left. An hour later, a rehab center called and told me they had a bed for him, and they would come and pick him up by 6 PM at the church. I waited, praying that he would come back. At 4:01 the elevator door opened, and there was Oscar. He was so relieved when

I told him about the call. I bought him dinner at the pizza shop next door, and we came back to the church to wait. He was exhausted, and fell asleep in a chair, waking up once from a sound sleep to say "Gracias, pastora," and dozed off again. When the driver got there to pick him up, I asked Oscar my customary question, "Would you like a hug or a handshake?" He, like most, opted for the hug. When Oscar got into the car, he was as giddy as a child going on vacation. He waved from the car until he was out of sight.

Reflection: Oscar's story is certainly one that I will never forget. His words, "Pastora, I have put drugs before mi familia, food, my health, and my God" haunt me at times. I cannot imagine something having such a grip on my life that it would take precedence over everything else that matters to me. And yet, I could see how real that grip was on Oscar.

Ponderings: Think about the things that are most important to you. Does anything get in the way of your relationship or connection with those things? It may not be drugs or alcohol; perhaps it's work, or anger, or food, or other relationships.

Prayer: Merciful God, addiction is ugly and painful. We grieve that it is such a prevalent issue in our communities, and we pray for your guidance on how to work towards solutions. We pray for all those currently living with addictions. Give them courage and strength to move toward sobriety. Help them know that you will walk with them on the journey. We pray for all those who work with individuals living with addiction. Thank you for their dedication and strength to walk alongside folks during some of the most difficult moments of their lives. We ask you for empathy and attitudes free of judgement for those who are struggling; help us to be part of the solution by loving as you love. **Amen.**

"The days aren't so bad, but the nights get lonely"

Scripture Verse: "I lie awake; I am like a lonely bird on the housetop." – Psalm 102:7 (NRSV)

Story: I met Scott* after our first monthly prayer walk. Four of us had gathered to walk through the city and pray for the people who live, work, and play there. We took along blessing bags, small tote bags filled with toiletries, snacks, socks, a bottle of water, and a list of community resources. Each bag also had a little information about the church. If we saw people on our walk who looked as if they could use the bag, we would strike up a conversation and offer one to them. I don't remember meeting Scott during the walk, but I do remember the note that was stuck in the front door of the church later that day, thanking us for the blessing bag. It said, "Thank you to who gave me the bag, it is very nice! God bless you all! From, Scott."

Scott began stopping by the office regularly, and occasionally attending worship. He has been homeless here in Lancaster for about a year and a half. He is intelligent and witty with an incredible sense of humor and a wealth of music and pop culture knowledge. He is also kind, polite, and generous. He struggles with mental illness that makes it difficult for him to maintain a permanent housing situation. He visits the office a few times a week, mostly to get a cup of coffee and to talk. He often dozes off, both in the office and at worship, because this is a safe space for him, and safe spaces can be hard to find.

One day he came in, and he was not his usual pleasant self. I asked what was wrong, and he told me that he was tired. He then corrected himself and said, "I'm not just tired, I'm weary; I've been on the streets for over a year now, and I'm just weary. The days aren't so bad because you walk around and you can be just like everyone else, but the nights get lonely. I haven't had a girlfriend in several years. The streets just aren't the place to start that type of relationship. There's nowhere to go for privacy and how do you make that work? I mean, I'm not looking for just, you know, sex. I want someone to talk to and be with." My heart hurt as I listened and watched him.

The weariness was evident on his face and in his words. His desire for human companionship felt out of his reach. I could think of no words that would help, so I sat quietly and listened. After a minute or so, I said, "Scott, I can only imagine how difficult all of this must be. Is there something I can do to support you in your weariness?" He asked for prayer, and although my words felt inadequate, we prayed that he might feel God walking with him in his weariness. I felt that praying for him to be freed from his weariness would somehow minimize the depth of the sorrow he was feeling, sorrow that did not come overnight and likely would not leave overnight. So instead, we prayed that God would meet him in that weariness, offering him companionship and connection.

Reflection: Scott's words caused me to reflect on the difference between being tired and being weary. The distinction was important to him.

Ponderings: When's the last time that you felt not just tired, but weary? How did God meet you in your weariness?

Prayer: God of our tiredness and weariness, it is when we are at our most weary that we often feel the most distant from you. Help us feel your nearness; remind us that you are with us even in the darkest night. Help us to let your presence shine through us for those who are experiencing loneliness and exhaustion. Remind us of your time in the wilderness, so that we may remember that we are not alone. **Amen.**

"I'd like to take you to Red Lobster"

Scripture Verse: "Don't keep hoarding for yourselves earthly treasures that can be stolen by thieves. Material wealth eventually rusts, decays, and loses its value. – Matthew 6:19 (TPT)

Story: Abner* is an alcoholic. He knows he's an alcoholic. His fear of getting help still outweighs his fear of dying from alcohol abuse. He tells me that if he doesn't get help, he will drink himself to death. He stands on the corner with a sign that says "homeless," "hungry," or "anything helps" depending on the day. One day, while stopped at the red light, I rolled down my window and gave him my card. I told him he could come see me in the office and I could help him to get a meal. He came by and told me his story. He had a wicked sense of humor that he used as a defense mechanism to deal with the tougher parts. He was open and honest, but matter of fact. He didn't really believe that any program would truly help him, but nonetheless, he asked if I could help him explore his rehab options. After we had discussed all the possibilities, he said, "I'll come back, but today, I'm just not ready." I assured him that he was welcome back anytime, ready or not.

I often drive by the spot where he stands, and I usually wave and say hello. If I get the red light, I'll ask how he's doing. He always says, "Not as good as you!" and laughs. One day he came over to my car and said, "Do you know what I'd like to do? I'd like to take you to Red Lobster. I'd like to take you there and let you get whatever you want off the menu." I thanked him for his thoughtfulness and told him that I would like for him to use the money he gets to buy himself something good to eat. And he said, "Well yes, but if I had the money, that's what I'd like to do." I smiled at his generosity, knowing he meant what he said, and I thanked him again. This warmed my heart far more than any clam chowder or cheddar biscuits could.[1]

---

[1]After writing this story, I learned that Abner died on the streets from alcohol consumption. Without a support system, there was no obituary. To my knowledge, there was no memorial service. One line appeared in the monthly autopsy report in the newspaper, and a bag of cheddar biscuits from Red Lobster was shared among friends in his memory at a church potluck. One woman, while eating her biscuit, laughed and said, "Abner got it right; when I die, I want people to eat something good in my memory."

Reflection: Abner's brutal honesty is jarring and his fear is real. He drinks to numb the pain he is feeling. Rehab isn't going to take that away; it will force him to face it. Even if I think that Abner should get help, it has to wait until he is ready. I can't force him, but what I can do is love him and encourage him every step of the way. I hope that by showing Abner that my acceptance is not based on his sobriety, I am showing him what God's unconditional love is like.

Ponderings: How could you show gratitude and hospitality without spending even a dollar? What would you do to show your gratitude to someone if money were no object? Who are you so grateful for that you would give beyond your means to express that gratitude? Have you told that person?

Prayer: God of all, today we remember the widow and her two little coins that she gave away, even though it was all that she had. Make us as generous as she and Abner were. Help us to remember to freely express our gratitude and let people know how much they mean to us. Remind us that generosity with our words can be just as powerful, and often more powerful, than the generosity of our wallets. **Amen.**

"I'd like to confess…"

Scripture Verse: "You will never succeed in life if you try to hide your sins. Confess them and give them up; then God will show mercy to you." – Proverbs 28:13 (GNT)

Story: Jackson* was friends with the previous pastor. A big man with an even bigger heart, he stopped in for a visit shortly after he heard there was a new pastor at the church. He came in and asked to see the pastor, and was startled to learn that the church had hired a woman. He was part of the Orthodox tradition, and he wasn't sure how he felt about talking to me. He said, "Well I was really hoping to come and confess to the new pastor. Can I do that? Can I confess to you?" We found a quiet place to sit, and I explained that as this was a Protestant Church, he didn't have to confess to me, but could confess to God directly. We could certainly talk about what was on his heart, and then we could pray together about it.

He seemed to like that idea, and he opened up about a relationship that he was struggling with. We talked for quite some time and then we prayed about it together. After our prayer, I explained that asking for forgiveness from God was important, but so was seeking out forgiveness from the person or persons we had hurt. Jackson asked me if I would call the offended party and tell that person that he had come for confession about his wrong doings. I explained why that didn't feel appropriate to me, and encouraged him to talk to this person directly. He practically begged me to make the call. I told him I would sit in the room with him while he called, if that would be helpful.

He dug out his phone and dialed the number, and when the person answered, Jackson said, "My pastor is here with me and wants to tell you something." I was really startled, and I don't remember exactly what I said to put the responsibility back on him, but I did. I was feeling irritated with his "antics" until after he got off the phone. He thanked me and smiled. He hadn't meant to be sneaky or pushy. He just got scared and froze at the last minute. Afterwards, Jackson visited me every few weeks, and each time he would tell me how good that relationship has been going. He never again mentioned his concern about my being a female pastor.

Reflection: Jackson had been used to confessing his sins to a priest who would then pray to God on his behalf. I could have sent him away to a priest to do that, but I sensed that he was also really looking for a safe space to speak his guilt out loud. As human beings, we all know the feelings of shame and guilt. I believe that is precisely why it is helpful for us to talk to others about the things that cause those feelings. God wants us to be free from these burdens and has assured us of Her forgiveness when we go to Her with a repentant heart. Perhaps that is one of the reasons we live in community with one another.

Ponderings: Have you ever been in a situation where you found comfort by confessing your wrongdoing to another person? Has anyone ever unburdened their heart to you by sharing something he or she was feeling guilty about?

Prayer: Most merciful God, thank you for the gifts of grace and forgiveness. Thank you, Jesus, for your willingness to come and live here with us on earth, so that we may be in direct and personal relationship with you. Remind us that there is nothing that we can't talk to you about, no matter what we have done to distance ourselves from you. God, thank you for the gift of a community of believers with whom we can talk and pray with honestly. Assure us that your desire for us is to be free from guilt and shame that seek to weigh us down and further distance us from Your joy. **Amen.**

"It's hard to feel clean"

Scripture Verse: When a woman has a discharge of blood that is her regular discharge from her body, she shall be in her impurity for seven days, and whoever touches her shall be unclean until the evening. Everything upon which she lies during her impurity shall be unclean; everything also upon which she sits shall be unclean. – Leviticus 15:19–20 (NRSV)

Story: It was a hot summer day, and I was secretly regretting that I had said that our monthly prayer walks would happen regardless of the weather. Binn's park was our next stop, and as we arrived, we found three women sitting on benches. We chatted with them for a few minutes and offered them blessing bags. The bags contained water, socks, snacks, tissues, toiletries, and a few other items. Sarah* asked me if we happened to have any powder. I told her we didn't. She looked down at her feet and said, "OK."

She quickly looked back up again and said, "You know, because it's hard to feel clean on the streets, especially on the hot days. There's nowhere to go to get out of the heat, and you end up in the same clothes without anywhere to shower. Especially when you have your period. It's just gross. At night we don't really have access to bathrooms, and during that time of the month it's even harder. You just can't feel clean. And if you don't have any money, what are you supposed to do about feminine products? There's not really anything you can do about it, but it's just hard."

I am glad that I was able to continue speaking calmly with Sarah, because her bold vulnerability startled me to my core. I promised her that if she could come to the office the following Monday, we would have feminine products and powder for her, but that hardly seemed like enough. I had picked up little cues about what would be helpful in a blessing bag from other people on the street. Small resealable plastic bags are useful because people are carrying their birth certificates and social security cards, which are not waterproof. Socks are like gold because protecting one's feet is essential when you are outside walking all day in every type of weather. Instant coffee packets are appreciated because, well, it's coffee. Simple first aid items like band aids and antiseptic wipes come in handy because cuts and scrapes happen often and they can get infected easily.

Sarah's sharing gave me a glimpse into her world and the world of so many others. We are so quick to shy away from talking about menstruation because it is seen as dirty and unclean, and it seemed like for a split second, Sarah wasn't going to say anything either. I know it took a lot of courage for her to tell a group of strangers about this need, but she did. And because she did, we now keep a supply of feminine products including tampons, pads, wipes, and yes, powder, in the office. Her vulnerability and advocacy allowed us to bless at least a dozen women with these items.

Reflection: Sarah's story is one of the most humbling I have experienced in my ministry. She opened my eyes and increased my compassion profoundly. Her willingness to express her need for feminine hygiene products to strangers, in spite of her discomfort with such a personal topic, led to her own needs being met as well as those of other women. I hope that I see her again to tell her what an impact she has had.

Ponderings: Have you ever had an eye-opening experience while listening to someone's story? How did it impact or change your life? Have you ever told that person how much it meant to you?

Prayer: Giver of birth to every living thing, we praise you for the miracle that is procreation. We ask you to remove the shame and stigma associated with menstruation. Help us to see it as a natural part of the cycle of life, a part of our human existence. Thank you for people who, like Sarah, speak up to raise awareness of the struggles of others on a variety of issues, including feminine hygiene when homeless. Open our ears and eyes so we may walk alongside her and others, offering whatever support we can. **Amen.**

"I'm not going to follow rules that deny my humanity!"

Scripture Verse: "As God's loving servants, you should live in complete freedom, but never use your freedom as a cover-up for evil. Recognize the value of every person and continually show love to every believer. Live your lives with great reverence and in holy awe of God. Honor your rulers." – 1 Peter 2:16–17 (TPT)

Story: Margo* was angry and rough around the edges. She cursed frequently and threatened to beat up anyone who messed with her. I was there when she was banned for a week from the breakfast program for threatening clients. I was a little concerned when she showed up at the church several weeks later, looking for assistance to get a replacement state ID card. Her guard was up, and it took a while for her to relax. I was quick to see that her tough and angry façade was one of self-protection. As a young, homeless, transgender woman of color, she has had to be. To be honest, I was amazed that she opened up to me as quickly as she did. She was struggling, and didn't know where to turn or what to do. She had burned some bridges, and some of the traditional shelter options were not available to her because she was transgender.

Margo explained that at one shelter, she had been forced to shower and bunk with the men. She tried staying there, but was harassed and made to feel uncomfortable. She was not allowed to wear her skirts because they offended others. She was given "more appropriate" clothes to wear. She began to feel depressed, angry, and later unsafe. When she refused to abide by the bathroom rules laid out for her, she was asked to leave the program. She said she knew that that would happen, but she realized that she couldn't stay there anyway. She said she couldn't continue to follow rules that denied her humanity. She also shared that she felt safer on the streets.

After a few setbacks, we were able to get her a duplicate ID. I didn't see her for a few months, and I worried that something bad might have happened to her. One day, she rang the doorbell at the church, and I almost didn't recognize her. She wore a lovely coat, her hair and her nails were done, and she had the biggest smile on her face. She was on her way to catch the bus, but had a few minutes to talk. She wanted me to know that she had used that ID to get a job, and she was no longer living on the streets. She also told me that she had decided that she was not going to spend time with negative people who brought her down, and that she'd like to find a way to share her story to help others who might be struggling. First, she wanted to find a second job. Her current job provided enough to cover her bills, but she wanted to have some money to do fun stuff too. She was beyond giddy to share that news with me, and truth be told, after feelings of relief washed over me, I was giddy for her too. What a transformation!

Reflection: I felt powerless to help Margo at first. We could get her the ID, but it would take time, and she was living on the street. She was tough and people were afraid of her, but I questioned her safety. I didn't feel like I had done much at all for her. I was overjoyed when she came back to tell me she was doing well. She told me she was grateful for all my help. It was a gentle reminder to me that we cannot place a value on offering safe space for people to let down their guard and share their stories. It takes commitment and time, but it can be extremely powerful. We must also never underestimate the power of prayer. Margo never wanted to pray with me, but she did appreciate my prayers for her.

Ponderings: Have you ever been asked or told to do something that went against your personal or ethical convictions like Margo was when she was asked to give up her skirts or sleep in the men's section of the shelter? What did you do?

Prayer: God of all, help us to see people for who they truly are. Help us to see past the smokescreens and protective walls that people put around themselves. Let us be the safe space where they are able to tear down those walls. Help us to help people walk in their own humanity, whatever that looks like. Remind us each day that simple acts of kindness and generosity really can change the world. **Amen.**

"Maybe I can wash your windows?"

Scripture Verse: "There are different kinds of service, but the same Lord. There are different kinds of working, but in all of them and in everyone it is the same God at work." – 1 Corinthians 12:5–6 (NIV)

Story: Brett* saw me outside lugging bags into the lobby of our building and asked me if he could help. I was grateful, as I still had a few cases of water and was not looking forward to hauling them into the elevator and then to my office. He made it look easy as he picked up the rest of my items. We reached the office and I showed him where to stash the water and bags. I had seen him hanging around the bus station a few times, and I asked him where he was from. He's a Lancaster native, but after a fight with the mother of his children, he was out on the street. He didn't have a job at the moment, but he was looking. I gave him some leads on some jobs and he said he would check them out.

Our conversation ended, but he continued to linger. I could tell there was something else he wanted to say. Finally, he said, "Do you have any other work I can do?" I told him there wasn't anything that I could think of off the top of my head, but why was he asking? He confessed that he was hungry and didn't have money for food, but he didn't want a handout. I tried to give him a Subway gift card as a thank you for helping me carry my stuff in, but he said that was too much. He said, "Maybe I could wash your windows, or sweep the stairs, or something? Just give me something to do worth as much as that gift card." I racked my brains; the windows had just been done the week prior, and I wasn't sure if any clients would use the stairs in the next hour.

Eventually, I asked him if he was available on Sunday morning. We would need to put all the furniture back in place after the floor cleaners finished on Saturday. He said he would absolutely come back, so I gave him the gift card, and he left. True to his word, he showed up right on time on Sunday morning. However, a group of members had come in later on Saturday evening and had reset all the furniture, not realizing that Brett and I had made an arrangement. I explained what had happened, and Brett and I chuckled about it. He chose to stay for worship, and returned again the following week. He reminded me that he was still available to wash the windows and do some other cleaning. If he comes in again, we'll try to have something lined up for him.

Reflection: Brett is a hard worker who hates being idle. He is the opposite of the stereotype that many conjure up when they think about what it is to be homeless. He is kind, yet insistent about earning his keep. Many people like Brett are one pay check or life trauma away from homelessness.

Ponderings: Has Brett's story, or any of the others in the past three weeks, caused you to question what you thought about poverty and homelessness? What insights have you gained, and will they impact how you live out your witness in the world?

Prayer: God of all learning, growth, and wisdom, we thank you for putting people in our paths who challenge our assumptions and make us see the world with a wider lens. Stretch us and our worldview so we become more aware of your creation and plan. Open us to new ideas and give us courage to turn these new insights into actions for your glory. **Amen!**

"After all you've done, now you're going to serve me?"

Scripture Verse: "Who is more important, the one who sits at the table or the one who serves? The one who sits at the table, of course. But not here! For I am among you as one who serves." – Luke 22:27 (NLT)

Story: Richie* was big on appetite but low on money. I found him arguing with himself outside the church on bazaar day. As I was greeting passersby, I asked Richie how he was doing. He said, "Well miss, I'd be doing better if I had a job, but I can't get a job, so I guess I'm not so good." I asked him what sort of work he was looking for, and he argued with himself again before answering, "Anyplace that will hire me." He was rubbing his hands together like he was cold, so I invited him in for a cup of coffee. He looked longingly at the food and I asked if he could eat a hot dog. He said, "Sure, but I don't have any money because I don't have a job." I ordered him two hot dogs and sent him to sit down and wait for them.

Now let me introduce you to a compassionate and comical member of our congregation who often takes on the role of grill master at church events where hot dogs are on the menu. He was on duty at the church bazaar that day. He was wearing his Vietnam Veteran's hat that I had seen him wear so many times before. He brought Richie his hot dogs and asked him what he usually put on them. Ritchie looked at him and must have noticed his hat because he asked the man if he had served in the war. Our grill master jokingly said, "Yes, but now I take my orders from her," pointing at me. I feigned shock, but couldn't help laughing. The grill master repeated his question. "Can I get you anything for on your hot dogs?"

Richie's eyes got big and he said, "No man, no. That's not right, after all you've done to serve this country and now you are going to serve me? I mean, no, I can't believe this, you're really going to serve me. Thank you for your service. You served in the war, and now here you are serving me my hot dogs. I just can't believe this. She buys my food, and you bring it out to me. That's just not right man. Wow! You served me. Thank you! Thank you so much man." As the event progressed, Richie became more comfortable and talked with more people in the congregation, including a few more comical exchanges with our grill master.

Reflection: It's hard as a pastor to think about this story and not think about Jesus washing the feet of the disciples before he was arrested. It's also hard to be a person who is passionate about social justice and not note that Richie is a black man and our grill master is white. It's also important to point out that so many veterans who served in Vietnam did not come home feeling as if their service was appreciated or that their sacrifice was honored. Any of these on their own would have made this a beautiful story, but all three together make it nothing short of a God moment.

Ponderings: When has someone who you saw as a person of honor or a person to be respected served you or done something kind for you? What impact did that have?

Prayer: God of surprising moments, thank you for providing us with glimpses of your grace shared between your people. We thank you for all those who have sacrificed so much to serve their countries through military service as a means of protecting our freedoms. May they never feel as if their service were not appreciated and valued. God help us to express our gratitude, surprise, and joy with the passion that Richie did. Give us courage to be bold and lavish in our expressions of praise. **Amen.**

"Can I have another hug?"

Scripture Verse: "Holy Embraces all around! All the churches of Christ send their warmest greetings." – Romans 16:16 (MSG)

Story: Research shows that receiving hugs every day can improve the quality of a person's life and actually promote specific health benefits. Not surprisingly, most people don't get the required number of hugs to obtain the full effect. This is especially true for individuals who are homeless. Early on during my time at this church, I started doing something very simple that has had an impact on my ministry. The last question I ask a person I am working with is "Are you a hug or a handshake kind of person?" I wish I had thought to keep statistics on the responses, but a vast majority, maybe even as high as 90%, choose the hug.

Some have said, "Whichever you want." And after I put the choice back on them, they usually opt for the hug. Others shy away a bit and tell me that they haven't showered in a while and are afraid they stink. And after I assure them that I am not worried about that, they too, often reach out for a hug. Some are tentative and quick. Others latch on and don't let go. Every now and then, the hug prompts tears. One thing is clear, the offer of a hug is meaningful to so many. It was certainly meaningful to Angel.*

His story, sadly, is not unique. Angel was abused at home and ran away to stay with friends. He ended up on the streets and was trying to figure out how to put his life back together. I shared some community resources with him, and our conversation wound down. I asked him if he was a hug or handshake kind of guy, and after a brief pause, he said, "I'll take a hug." I gave him a hug, and he headed for the door. With his hand on the doorknob, he asked me if I knew where he could go to get some clothes. I pulled out a community connections sheet and highlighted the places that offered clothing. I also pointed out some places he may want to reach out to for a few other things.

He started to walk to the door again, and I sat back down behind my desk. When I looked up, he was once again standing in front of my desk. He sheepishly looked at me and said, "I was wondering if I could have another hug?"

Reflection: Physical contact is essential to human development. A newborn is placed on its mother's chest to feel close to her. We snuggle and cuddle with babies, and we offer comfort and love to children through hugs. We often think that this need is only true for babies and small children, but it's not. Even as adults we can crave the touch of another human being, especially when we are struggling. We might hold hands, pat someone on the shoulder, embrace, give a high five, or shake someone's hand, all forms of physical contact that help to make us feel better.

Ponderings: When's the last time you received or gave a good hug? I invite you to close your eyes and linger in that memory for a moment.

Prayer: Almighty God, touch us with your spirit. Open us to feel Your arms around us in an embrace that matches any circumstance we might be experiencing. If we are weary, may we come to you and fall into an embrace filled with peace and rest. If we are excited, let us find you dancing with us in an embrace of jubilation. Be what we need in this moment, so that we can have the strength and courage to meet the needs of others who are desperately yearning to feel your touch. **Amen.**

"I'd say that's Him in me, wouldn't you?"

Scripture Verse: "Do you not know that you are God's temple and that God's Spirit dwells in you?... For God's temple is holy, and you are that temple." – 1 Corinthians 3:16,17b (NRSV)

Story: This is a second story about Scott,* a man I met after our very first prayer walk (see the December 16 entry). Scott has been coming to see me regularly for several months, and we have talked about almost every topic under the sun. Scott doesn't have much in the way of a faith background, but we have talked about scripture or about the nature of God a few times. These times are rare, so when he mentions something about God, it takes me by surprise. On one particularly difficult day, Scott found out that yet another possible housing situation had fallen through. I told him I was sorry, and he said, "Don't worry about me, I'll be alright. Something will come through for me."

I wondered how he maintained such a positive attitude in light of all his challenges. I said, "Scott, I don't get it. How do you still keep such a generous, caring attitude and such a wonderful sense of humor when things are so difficult?" He shrugged his shoulders, pointed up toward the ceiling and said, "I guess I'd say that's Him in me, wouldn't you?" It took a moment for his words to register, maybe because of how simply they had been spoken. As if it were common knowledge. And on some level, maybe it was. But there is nothing common about the spirit of this man who has been forced to leave almost every establishment in a three-block radius, charged with loitering. There is nothing common about his maintaining a generous and pleasant demeanor when his feet are blistered and infected from past frostbite and a lack of means to take care of them. There is nothing common about this man who has no family and only meager community support still believing that something is going to come through for him.

Reflection: Perhaps Scott's uncommonness is precisely how we know he was speaking the truth. The goodness in him is none other than God! Instead of displaying the pain, anger, frustration, and feelings of resignation caused by years of things going wrong, Scott reflects the light and love of God. The God we worship can almost always be found in the unexpected: He dined with tax collectors; He touched lepers; and He verbally sparred with a Samaritan woman. So yes, Scott, I am absolutely certain that the love I see in you is the love of this very same God who was born to a teenage, unwed woman and a carpenter; who came in the form of a baby who would spend his first nights sleeping amidst barnyard animals and was welcomed by farmhands and nobles alike. Yes, indeed, that is the same God that is living in you, my friend.

Ponderings: Who do you know who exemplifies God's Spirit in some way? What is it about them that makes you believe that?

Prayer: God who dwells within each one of us, allow us to see you in others, and allow us to see you in ourselves. Use that vision to open our hearts and minds to love others and ourselves the way we love you. Remind us that you go with us on every step of this journey. On this Christmas Eve, we remember that you came to earth in the form of a baby for that very purpose. Thank you for that gift! **Amen!**

"I ain't never known love like this before"

Scripture Verse: "Above all, constantly echo God's intense love for one another deeply, for love will be a canopy over a multitude of sins." – 1 Peter 4:8 (TPT)

Story: I met Ron* on the sidewalk the day of the church bazaar. I watched him go into the bus station and very quickly come out again. He was muttering to himself about being cold. I introduced myself and told him he could stand in our lobby to warm up if he wanted to. I asked if he drank coffee, and he nodded, so I invited him to come upstairs for a cup of hot coffee and some breakfast. He ate two hot dogs, and then two more. People greeted him and talked to him as if he were a friend. Even though they had never met him before. Even though he was black, and they were white. Even though he was loud and a bit rough around the edges and they were a bit more reserved. Even though his clothes were dirty and torn. They served him food and drink and invited him to come back anytime. An older member of the congregation told him that he was to come as he is. She patted him on the hand and said, "We aren't the type to care if you've got nice clothes to wear to church. That certainly wouldn't matter to God, so why should it matter to us?"

Throughout each of these exchanges, he just kept saying over and over again, "Wow, you all are so nice. I ain't never seen love like this before. I ain't never known love like this before." I was both moved and saddened by this statement. Moved that he felt loved at our church, and sad that this was a novel experience for him. I said to him, "Ron, I sure am glad that you are feeling so much love here, but I'm also really sorry that you don't feel it more often in other places. I believe God calls us to love all people all the time." Ron looked at me for a moment, seemingly searching for words. Then he said, "Miss, you might be right about how God wants us to treat others, but most folks, they ain't got the memo." I felt those words touch the deepest part of my being, and I stammered some sort of response like, "I hear you." He started talking to someone else, and I slipped away with his words ringing in my ears. "I ain't never known love like this before."

Reflection: Today is Christmas, the day we celebrate the birth of our Savior, Jesus Christ. This is one instance where we all can say that we have never known love like this before. God has done the amazing, the remarkable, the unfathomable. God has chosen to come and live with us, to walk beside us, to take on all that it means to be human so that God can draw closer in relationship with us and that our mutual love can continue to grow. I wonder, on this celebratory day, what can I do to help others get the memo?

Ponderings: When have you "missed the memo" about loving and serving your neighbors? Have you ever been overwhelmed by God's love for all of Her creation?

Prayer: God of love, thank you for this gift that we can't fully comprehend or imagine. As we peek into the manger, give us the wonder of Ron as we say, "We've never known love like this before." Give us the words to speak as we share this love throughout the world, making sure that others "get the memo" of who You are. You are pure, unbridled, boundless, and complete Love. **Amen.**

Conclusion

Hope. Something positive is going to happen. A desire will be met. An expectation will come to fruition. There are better days ahead. There is good in the world. I am grateful for many opportunities to provide a bit of hope, and I am even more grateful for the many ways that my interactions with others prove to be hope-filled experiences for me. The stories in this devotional are just a few examples of interactions that have happened in the two years since I have been called to serve at Moravian Center of Lancaster. This devotional focuses on those interactions I have had specifically with individuals who asked for assistance. I could have just as easily created a similar book with hope-filled interactions with congregation members, or with clients and staff of the adult day center. The Moravian Center of Lancaster is a place filled with hope from many different angles.

In my role as pastor and social worker, I often find myself advocating for the people I serve. I may speak with the individuals who make decisions that impact community service programs. I may try to improve those programs and activities themselves. But most of my work is done through everyday conversations with friends, colleagues, neighbors, family members, and acquaintances. In sharing these stories, I hope to "prove" that very few homeless people are lazy. I hope to offer examples of the ways that the system is broken and how it sometimes causes more harm than good. I also hope to point out places and programs that are getting it right and are working to solve problems of poverty, addiction, and homelessness, while encouraging each person to do their part.

A large part of advocacy work is giving a voice to those who may not have opportunities to be heard otherwise. I love being able to do that, and I pray that I have adequately done justice to the stories of each person represented in these pages. My desire is that you have experienced a renewed sense of hope and love through the readings of these stories. That in some way the scriptures, stories, reflections, and prayers, have deepened your connection to God, to humanity, and/or to the hope within you. I pray that you have found Christ's love somewhere among these pages. As we have moved through the expectant season of Advent into Christmas, let us celebrate that our deepest anticipations, expectations, longings and hopes have been revealed through the story of a family sleeping in a cave where animals were fed because no beds were available to them. If that isn't a sign that hope comes in all shapes and sizes and ways, what is?

If you ever find yourself in the heart of Lancaster city, stop by and visit us at "Your Friendly Neighborhood Hope Shop"!

Merry Christmas!
Mandy

The following translations of Scripture have been used:

GNT – Good News Translation
MSG – The Message
NIV – New International Version
NLT – New Living Translation
NRSV – New Revised Standard Version
TPT – The Passion Translation

Appendix: Community Organizations

Most of the folks you have read about in these pages have been assisted in some way by the programs of Lanc Co MyHome. A portion of the proceeds from the sale of this book will go to support the work that they are doing in Lancaster, Pennsylvania, to ensure that those who are unsheltered are met with dignity and love. The staff and volunteers of Lanc Co MyHome and the organizations they partner with certainly have gotten the memo about the importance of loving each other. Please read more (below) about Lanc Co MyHome and some of the organizations they partner with in the Lancaster Community. Most of the information shared about these organizations is taken directly from their websites. I encourage you to go to the provided links to get more information. I also invite you to prayerfully consider additional ways you can offer your support.

Lanc Co MyHome

Lanc Co MyHome is a network of organizations and individuals working together to provide all the people experiencing homelessness within our community with shelter and a place to stay. Lanc Co MyHome is a 160+ partner-strong coalition serving the Lancaster County community since 2009. Made up of service providers, public officials, government agencies, healthcare providers, private sector businesses, emergency response teams, faith-based organizations/churches, behavioral health agencies, and school districts, Lanc Co MyHome prides itself on the broad reach of its partners across all sectors. In 2019, our network collectively served in excess of 4,000 individuals, including families and children, throughout the county.

Through regular communication coalition-wide data measures, Lanc Co MyHome has shown significant positive impact in this community. Penn Medicine Lancaster General Health hosts the dedicated staff of the coalition, providing a strong organizational backbone. Lanc Co MyHome is one of the only homeless coalitions in the Commonwealth of Pennsylvania that has dedicated staffing who provide support to the coalition partners.

Collective impact and embracing diversity in the coalition has led to innovations such as a focus on prevention, utilizing school districts as strong partners to address student and family poverty and homelessness. Other notable innovations include eviction prevention programs that have provided data showing that the community can prevent homelessness and a collaborative funding platform that combines several funding streams (federal, state, local, and private) and allows all of those funds to be awarded through one application, thus making acquiring funds easier for providers and partners. In 2019, Lanc Co MyHome partners realized several drop-in centers, another innovation that is pulling together a broad cross-section of the community to provide services to individuals in need.

Homelessness is not an individual struggle, but an opportunity for a community to join together and create a strong partnership based upon care, concern, and the well-being of our neighbors. Our clients' resiliency, our partners' passion, and our community's generosity has made Lancaster a national leader in how homelessness is resolved. Together with individuals, groups, organizations, and corporations, we continue to strive to make homelessness in Lancaster rare, brief, and non-recurring. To learn more about how you can help, visit http://lanccomyhome.org/en-US/get-involved.

United Way of Lancaster County

United Way of Lancaster County advances the education, economic mobility, and health of our community by mobilizing resources, people, and organizations. United Way works to solve our county's biggest social service issues by bringing a variety of organizations together and providing financial and other resources.

In 2004, United Way of Lancaster County's Community Needs Committee published *The State of Housing and Homelessness*, the catalyst that launched what is now known as LancCo MyHome.

We continue to provide matching funds that enables the Coalition to bring hundreds of thousands of federal dollars to Lancaster County. We also provide seed funding for new and innovative partnerships that share our vision of an equitable Lancaster County where every individual could succeed, and our entire community thrives as a result.

In addition, we provide county-wide programs to support and engage our community members:

- Our Volunteer Income Tax Assistance (VITA) program provides free tax prep services by IRS-trained volunteers at numerous locations across the county for individuals and households that earn less than $62,000. By eliminating the cost of a paid tax service, we are able to keep more hard-earned money in the pockets of those who need it most.

- Our PA 211 East Call Center is a 24/7/365 helpline for those in need of guidance on where to find local resources. From food banks to health clinics to legal aid and more, our trained professional staff offers compassionate service via phone, text, or chat to those who don't know who to turn to for help. Dial 2-1-1 or text your zip code to 898-211.
- Our Get Connected Volunteer Center is an online "matching" system for community members who want to get involved in our community and the non-profit agencies that are looking for assistance.

To support the work of community partnerships and our own programming, we raise funds and mobilize other resources via workplace campaigns, corporate gifts, grants, events, and individual donors. In response to the pandemic, we partnered to raise and distribute $1 million extra dollars to support local COVID relief efforts. We also launched Project SOS – Share Our Stimulus – as a way for people to donate their stimulus checks and provide direct relief to individuals. Companies interested in learning how to get involved can contact campaign@ uwlanc.org. Individuals can donate online anytime at uwlanc.org/donate. Visit uwlanc.org for more details.

Water Street Mission

Each day Water Street Mission seeks to go beyond providing basic needs such as food, clothing, and shelter. We invite each man, woman, and child to experience true restoration in all areas of life, leaving them restored to be restorers to those around them.

Water Street Mission offers five core ministries, all of which seek to further restoration in our community. In our Mission, we have our residential and emergency shelter programs for men, women and children experiencing homelessness. We provide an environment of hope and healing where at-risk neighbors can find a hand-up and restoration with God. Through Water Street Health Services, we offer medical, dental, and behavioral health care to individuals going through homelessness or struggling with poverty.

Our Outreach Center serves neighbors in our community by providing weekly groceries through a shopping experience. We aim to connect with each person who comes through our doors so they know they have local support, and people who care about them. Our programs also stem into serving the next generation, with the aim to provide restoration *at the root*. Wonder Club Early Learning Center, our daily Pre-K and Kindergarten school, provides a loving education for children from primarily low-income families. At an older age, Teen Haven focuses on youth in Lancaster City, launching them into a life of leadership and purpose.

wsm.org | (717) 393-7709 | contact@wsm.org | 210 S. Prince Street

CrossNet Ministries

CrossNet Ministries exists to offer help and hope in the name of Jesus by empowering people in eastern Lancaster County. Our four areas of focus include youth, social services, community, and food and nutrition. We offer programs that help people (children through adults) build relationships and build resources. Programs include a youth center, food pantry, mentor program, tutoring program, case management, housing programs, financial assistance, community meals, transportation ministry, home repair, after-school programs for kids, and more! It is our desire to see youth and adults empowered to build their resources and take steps out of poverty. CrossNet Ministries is grateful to partner with Lan Co MyHome to walk alongside people who are experiencing homelessness in Lancaster County. Our Social Services team supports those experiencing homelessness in eastern Lancaster County by connecting them to local and county-wide resources. Lanc Co MyHome is making a difference in the community and we are grateful for their support to make it possible to continue to serve.

To learn more or to get involved at CrossNet Ministries, please visit elancocross.org or contact our office at 717-355-2454.

Anchor Lancaster

Anchor Lancaster exists to provide no-cost meals 52 weeks a year, 5 days a week to Lancaster's low-income, unsheltered, and socially excluded populations with love. A free breakfast is served from 8:30 a.m. until 9:45 a.m. each weekday. Everyone and anyone may come to eat. A nutritious menu of hot, protein-filled food items, juice, milk, cereal, toast, fruit, and coffee is served each day. The average number of people served each day is 180 people. Showers for guests are also provided two days a week for those who sign up. For more information, visit anchorlancaster.org.

Factory Ministries

At The Factory Ministries, we believe that everyone's journey matters! Our social services department provides a relational and caring environment where adults who are under-resourced and struggling with poverty-related issues can find hope and help as they navigate through life. The Factory Ministries is committed to not enabling, changing, or judging those struggling with poverty. Instead, we empower individuals by helping them to not just focus on symptoms but to develop the resources they need to deal with root issues. Our goal is to create healthy, resilient, and self-sufficient people who not just survive but thrive in their communities. To do that, we offer intakes, assessments, triage, and resource development in six main areas: physical, emotional, relational, spiritual, intellectual, and financial.

The Factory Ministries at the Together Community Center
3293 Lincoln Highway East
Paradise, PA 17562
Phone:717.687.9594
Fax:717.260.3654
info@thefactoryministries.com

Moravian Center of Lancaster

When the Lancaster Moravian Church moved into the city and started the Moravian Center Adult Day, it was their goal to create a partnership between the congregation and the center. The Moravian Center of Lancaster currently includes the Moravian Center Adult Day Care and the Lancaster Moravian Congregation. They are not only a congregation, but also the visionaries behind this amazing program that serves so many in our community. The adult day program is not a stand-alone entity, either, and the space that is used by the church and the day program is one and the same. Exercise at 10 AM each week-day morning is done in the same space that we worship in on Sunday at 10 AM. Cookies and Conversation is held at the same tables where day center participants eat lunch.

We are always praying for God's guidance as to how we are called to be the hands and feet of Christ in Lancaster. We have found opportunities to live out that call by feeding folks in a variety of ways, including the community food distributions and a joint effort with Meals on Wheels that allows us to share frozen meals. We also pray with and get to know people during our monthly prayer walks. We partner with a local day center to provide bus passes for individuals who need transportation to job interviews, work, and appointments. Pastor Mandy meets regularly with persons who are looking for counseling or other forms of assistance. In many instances, she works with the community outreach workers to find the best possible outcomes. The congregation at Moravian Center of Lancaster recently began sharing space with the Islamic Community Center of Lancaster, an adventure where new opportunities to partner together in service are just beginning. For more information about the Moravian Center of Lancaster visit https://www.lancastermoravian.org/.

Tenfold

Tabor and LHOP are now Tenfold. With 80 years of collective expertise, we will continue to serve as your trusted community partner offering a broader continuum of services to address homelessness to affordable rental housing to homeownership, and the creation of new housing units through Tenfold Community Lending.

At Tenfold, we believe housing is at the center of a thriving community. Every day, our team walks alongside our clients, helping them take the next step to a brighter future. Our Emergency Housing services enable clients to unlock a new beginning toward housing stability, and our Supportive Housing services empower people to gain new skills so they can obtain and maintain permanent housing through long-term self-sufficiency.

Learn more by visiting Tenfold's website at www. WeAreTenfold.org.

Domestic Violence Services of Lancaster

Founded in 1976 as a program of the Community Action Partnership of Lancaster County, Domestic Violence Services (DVS) provides comprehensive services to over 1,500 adult and child victims of domestic violence annually. DVS also provides education, training, and community outreach services. DVS is member organization of the Pennsylvania Coalition Against Domestic Violence (PCADV).

DVS Services and Programs:

- **24-hour hotline and text line** offering emergency support, counseling, and referrals
- **Safe House, or emergency shelter** and supportive services with a capacity of 32 adults and children

- **Domestic Violence Legal Center** offers legal advocacy and representation in the Protection from Abuse process and for related civil legal matters
- **Empowerment Counseling** services for individuals and support groups
- **Economic Empowerment** programming to assist survivors to gain long-term economic stability
- **Children's Programming** including counseling, trauma-informed psychoeducational groups and recreational activities for resident children and teens
- **Bridge House** transitional housing services to help victims and their children make the transition from the Safe House to permanent housing
- **Information and Referrals** to community programs and resources
- **Community Education** activities for schools, churches, civic groups, clubs and organizations
- **Trainings** for professionals in the community
- **Volunteer and Internship** programs

Contact Us
24/hour Hotline: (717) 299-1249
Text SAFE to 61222
Business: (717) 299-9677
Web: www.caplanc.org/dvs
E-mail: Christine Gilfillan, Director cgilfillan@caplanc.org

Community Services Group

Community Services Group (CSG) was founded in 1972 and provides a comprehensive network of Mental Health, IDD, and Outreach Services that empower adults, children and families to reach their full potential. CSG believes in creating an environment that values and respects all people by providing services in a manner that promotes dignity, diversity, responsibility, integrity, and excellence. CSG is proud to be a Certified B Corporation that meets the highest standards of social and environmental responsibility. CSG provides a variety of specialized programs that are designed to meet the individual needs of people in our community while promoting independence and wellness.

One specialty program within CSG is Outreach Case Management. Individuals living with mental illness and experiencing homelessness receive assistance from an Outreach Case Manager who is knowledgeable about the supports, benefits, and services available in Lancaster County. Referrals and assistance are provided in a collaborative and expedited manner for supports such as: food, clothing, utility assistance, housing options, educational and vocational resources, financial benefits, mental and physical healthcare, and connection to natural community resources.

The Lancaster County community can show support for the homeless population by:

- Advocating for landlords to increase housing availability to all people, specifically those who are homeless.
- Volunteer your time to be a mentor and provide social support and encourage positive participation in the community.
- Donate to the following providers who dedicate their time and energy to positively impact the cycle of homelessness – Lan Co MyHome, Tenfold, CSG, and the Lancaster County Food Hub.
- Provide essential supplies for outreach case managers to distribute directly to individuals in need (sleeping bags, backpacks, men's tee shirts, feminine hygiene items, men's body sprays, dry shampoo).

To make a referral to CSG services or to reach the Case Management Outreach Program please call 877-907-7970.

Good Samaritan Services

Good Samaritan Services is an agency that provides a full continuum of care to individuals and families experiencing homelessness. We offer Emergency Shelters, Residential Housing, and Housing Support Services across Lancaster and Chester Counties. We serve around 400 men, women, and children every year.

We also offer a plethora of financial stability and personal development resources that holistically and effectively address the needs of participants who are enrolled at Good Sam.

To learn more about Good Sam go to www.goodsam-services.org or call 1 (888) 477-0025.

ECHOS

Through support from Lanc Co MyHome, ECHOS offers a variety of different programs, interventions, and resources to address both the immediate needs and long-term stability of our clients and community. ECHOS primarily serves individuals at risk for or are currently experiencing homelessness due to a variety of reasons, including insufficient income, absence of natural supports, crises, and systemic barriers. ECHOS services are provided across a continuum of care, ranging from Eviction Prevention to Permanent Supportive Housing. Additional resources include housing and related supports, individual and family assistance, case advocacy, emergency shelter, community education, employment assistance, and youth crisis counseling. At ECHOS, our professionally trained staff walk alongside individuals and families to offer support, enable stability in their lives, and equip them with the necessary tools to be successful.

To support our vital community services, ECHOS seeks both volunteers and financial partners. Specifically, the Elizabethtown Emergency Shelter takes between 150 and 200 volunteers to run each season efficiently and effectively. Volunteers can sign up for shelter operational shifts or donate hot meals or supplies. Additionally, ECHOS seeks to grow our financial partnerships to meet the growing needs of our community by strengthening and expanding our current services.

For more information on ECHOS programs, eligibility requirements, program enrollment, or partnering with ECHOS, please visit https://echoslancaster.org/, contact info@echoslancaster.org, or call us at 717-361-0740.

Biography

"I believe I love because I am loved, which
drives my commitment to be a channel for
people to believe they are worthy to receive,
demonstrate, and express that love, and to
be a support for them to discover how to live
into and out of that love."

Mandy M. Mastros is the pastor at the Moravian Center of Lancaster: Lancaster Moravian Church in Lancaster, Pennsylvania. She is the chaplain for the Moravian Center Adult Day Program, which serves seniors with memory support needs. She is currently serving as the president of the Downtown Ministerium, which includes clergy and community leaders from the downtown Lancaster region. Mandy serves on the boards of Moravian Manor

Communities and Lanc Co MyHome. She graduated in 2017 with her Masters of Divinity degree from Moravian Theological Seminary and with her Masters of Social Work degree from Marywood University. She was ordained in the Moravian Church in October of 2017. Mandy is a licensed social worker in the state of Pennsylvania. She has lived her entire life in Lancaster County and feels blessed to be serving in a community that for so long has been home to her. She lives with her ten-year-old rescue dog Edna. She is passionate about community connections and resource building, with the goal of making sure all God's children have access to basic necessities including housing, food, safety, and belonging. In her limited spare time, Mandy enjoys reading, cross-stitching, spending time with friends and loved ones, and singing.

Acknowledgements

I strongly believe that every time one person shares part of their story with a second person who is open to receiving it, God accepts an invitation to be in the exchange. I am humbled every time a person reveals part of his/her/their life journey with me. I am keenly aware of the courage and vulnerability it can take to talk about the traumas and challenges that make up this messy thing called life. I am grateful to all the individuals who shared the parts of their stories with me that appear in this book. And to all of those whose stories are waiting to be told.

The congregation at the Moravian Center of Lancaster knows what it is to be the hands and feet of Jesus. Their passion for and dedication to the people of the city of Lancaster is remarkable, and that is what allows me to spend so much time getting to know and love the people in these pages. I am beyond blessed to be called to serve and to serve with such an amazing group of people.

This book would not be possible without the generosity of a woman who helped to underwrite the publishing costs of this book. She too believes that these stories are meant to be heard. I am grateful for her kindness and monetary support.

Cathy Frey has been a long-time friend. I wonder if she knew what she was getting herself into when I asked her if she would help me with the copyediting. I am so glad she knows where all the commas belong and where they don't, and so much more! I appreciate her hard work to make things flow smoothly.

The publishing process got real for me when I saw the first draft of the cover design by Ann Malcolm. She took just a few sentences of description and created a visual representation of "The Hope Shop." I am glad to call her friend and to work with her on this project.

Jenn T. Grace and Bailly Morse from Publish Your Purpose Press made the publishing process easy and enjoyable. If I had known how painless they could make the process, I may have done it earlier.